Mastering TikTok Marketing in 2023

Proven Strategies for Achieving Results

Alex Westwood

TABLE OF CONTENTS

Introduction

Welcome to the world of TikTok marketing! In this book, we will delve into the intricacies of leveraging TikTok as a powerful marketing platform in 2023. With its explosive growth and immense popularity, TikTok has emerged as a dynamic space for brands and content creators to reach and engage with a global audience. Whether you are a business owner, marketer, or aspiring influencer, this book will equip you with the knowledge and strategies to harness the full potential of TikTok for marketing success.

Chapter 1

Understanding the Power of TikTok in the Digital Landscape

1.1 The Rise and Influence of TikTok

TikTok has taken the world by storm, captivating millions of users and reshaping the digital landscape. In this section, we will explore the rise and influence of TikTok and how it has revolutionized the way people create and consume content.

TikTok's journey began in 2016 when the Chinese company ByteDance launched the app under the name Douyin in China. It quickly gained popularity among Chinese users, offering a platform for short-form videos set to music. In 2017, ByteDance introduced TikTok to international markets, and it quickly gained traction, especially among younger audiences.

One of the factors contributing to TikTok's rapid rise is its innovative and engaging content format. Users can create short videos of up to 60 seconds, incorporating music, effects, filters, and various creative features. This format allows for quick and easy content creation, appealing to the short attention spans of today's digital users.

TikTok's influence goes beyond entertainment. It has become a cultural phenomenon, spawning viral trends, challenges, and even creating its own celebrities.

The app has given rise to a new breed of content creators who have amassed millions of followers and have become influential figures in their own right.

1.2 The Unique Features and User Demographics of TikTok

TikTok stands out from other social media platforms due to its unique features and user experience. One of the key features that sets TikTok apart is its sophisticated video editing tools. Users can easily add special effects, filters, and soundtracks to their videos, enhancing their creative expression. The extensive library of licensed music and sound bites provides users with a wide range of options to choose from.

Another distinguishing feature of TikTok is its algorithm-driven content discovery. The "For You" page, powered by a robust recommendation algorithm, delivers personalized content to users based on their preferences and engagement history. This algorithmic approach ensures that users are consistently exposed to content that aligns with their interests, increasing engagement and time spent on the app.

In terms of user demographics, TikTok has a predominantly young user base. It has gained significant popularity among Gen Z and millennials, who are known for their penchant for video-centric social media platforms. However, the user base is expanding to include users from older age groups as well, as TikTok's appeal continues to grow.

1.3 The Impact of TikTok on Online Marketing

TikTok's explosive growth and massive user base have made it a hotbed for marketing opportunities. Brands across industries have recognized the power of TikTok as a platform to reach and engage with their target audiences in new and exciting ways.

The authentic and creative nature of TikTok content has allowed brands to showcase their products or services in innovative ways. From user-generated content campaigns to influencer partnerships, TikTok offers a range of marketing avenues for brands to explore. The platform's emphasis on storytelling and visual appeal provides brands with an opportunity to connect with consumers on a deeper level.

TikTok has also disrupted traditional advertising formats with its native ad options. From in-feed ads to branded effects and hashtag challenges, brands have the opportunity to integrate their messaging seamlessly into the TikTok experience. This native approach to advertising ensures that brands can capture the attention and interest of users without feeling intrusive or disruptive.

The impact of TikTok on online marketing extends beyond brand promotion. It has also fueled the growth of influencer marketing, with TikTok creators becoming powerful influencers in their respective niches. Influencer collaborations on TikTok have proven to be highly effective in driving brand awareness, engagement, and even sales.

In conclusion, TikTok's rise and influence have transformed the digital landscape. Its unique features, engaging content format, and young user demographics make it a fertile ground for marketing opportunities.

Brands that understand and harness the power of TikTok can position themselves at the forefront of digital marketing, capturing the attention and loyalty of a global audience. In the subsequent chapters, we will delve deeper into TikTok marketing strategies and techniques to help you make the most of this powerful platform.

Chapter 2

Creating an Effective TikTok Marketing Strategy

2.1 Defining Your Brand Identity and Objectives on TikTok

In the fast-paced and highly competitive world of TikTok marketing, it's essential to start with a solid foundation. Defining your brand identity and objectives will not only guide your TikTok strategy but also ensure consistency in your messaging and resonate with your target audience.

When defining your brand identity on TikTok, start by examining your brand's unique selling proposition (USP). What makes your brand stand out from the competition? Identify the key values, attributes, and strengths that define your brand and align with the interests and preferences of your target audience. By understanding your brand's essence, you can create content that authentically represents your brand and attracts like-minded TikTok users.

Once your brand identity is established, it's time to set clear and measurable objectives for your TikTok marketing efforts. Are you looking to increase brand awareness, drive website traffic, generate leads, or boost sales?

Clearly defining your goals will allow you to track your progress and evaluate the success of your TikTok campaigns.

Remember to set specific targets and establish a timeline to keep yourself accountable and motivated.

2.2 Identifying and Understanding Your Target Audience

To effectively reach and engage your target audience on TikTok, you need to have a deep understanding of who they are. Conduct thorough market research to identify the demographics, interests, preferences, and behaviors of your target audience.

Start by analyzing your existing customer base to identify common characteristics and trends. Consider factors such as age, gender, location, and psychographic traits. Additionally, leverage TikTok's built-in analytics tools to gain valuable insights into your TikTok followers and their engagement with your content. This data will provide you with a wealth of information about your audience's demographics, engagement patterns, and content preferences.

Once you have a clear understanding of your target audience, it's time to tailor your TikTok content to resonate with them. Speak their language, address their pain points, and create content that aligns with their interests and aspirations. This targeted approach will increase the likelihood of capturing their attention, fostering a genuine connection, and ultimately driving meaningful engagement.

2.3 Crafting Compelling Content Ideas for TikTok

Creating compelling and engaging content is the heart of any successful TikTok marketing strategy. TikTok thrives on authentic, creative, and entertaining content that captures the attention of users and encourages them to engage and share.

To start, immerse yourself in the TikTok community and research the latest trends and popular content formats. Stay up to date with the challenges, dances, and memes that are gaining traction on the platform. While it's important to stay relevant and tap into popular trends, don't be afraid to infuse your unique brand personality and storytelling into your content. Authenticity is key in building a loyal and engaged following.

Experiment with different content types to keep your TikTok feed diverse and engaging. Explore educational videos, behind-the-scenes glimpses, product demonstrations, user-generated content, and storytelling. TikTok offers a variety of tools and effects to enhance your videos and make them visually appealing. Leverage these features to create eye-catching and memorable content that stands out from the crowd.

Remember to keep your content concise and attention-grabbing. TikTok's short-form video format demands quick and engaging content that captures viewers' attention within the first few seconds. Use compelling visuals, catchy captions, and captivating hooks to draw viewers in and encourage them to watch your videos till the end.

In conclusion, creating an effective TikTok marketing strategy requires a strong foundation based on defining your brand identity, understanding your target audience, and crafting compelling content. By aligning your brand's values with your TikTok presence, connecting with your target audience, and creating content that resonates, you can establish a strong TikTok presence and drive meaningful results for your brand. In the subsequent chapters, we will delve deeper into the various tactics and techniques to enhance your TikTok marketing strategy and take it to the next level.

Chapter 3

Optimizing Your TikTok Profile and Content

3.1 Setting Up and Optimizing Your TikTok Profile

Your TikTok profile serves as the face of your brand on the platform, so it's essential to set it up in a way that captures the attention of users and effectively communicates your brand identity. Here are some key steps to optimize your TikTok profile:

a) Choose a Username: Select a username that is memorable, relevant to your brand, and easy to spell. Ideally, it should align with your brand name or a variation of it.

b) Profile Picture: Use a high-quality and recognizable profile picture that represents your brand. This could be your logo, a product image, or a professional headshot if you are a personal brand.

c) Bio: Craft a compelling bio that succinctly describes your brand, its values, and what users can expect from your content. Use keywords and emojis to make it visually appealing and engaging.

d) Link: Utilize the link in your bio to direct users to your website, online store, or any other relevant landing page. Consider using a link shortener to save space and track clicks.

e) Category: Choose the most appropriate category for your TikTok profile to help users understand your niche and target audience.

f) Featured TikToks: Showcase your best and most engaging TikTok videos in the "Featured TikToks" section of your profile. This provides a snapshot of your content and encourages users to explore further.

g) Privacy Settings: Review and adjust your privacy settings based on your preferences and the nature of your content. Consider whether you want your videos to be publicly visible or limited to your followers.

3.2 Crafting Attention-Grabbing TikTok Captions and Hashtags

Captions and hashtags play a vital role in boosting the discoverability and engagement of your TikTok content. Here are some tips to optimize your captions and hashtags:

a) Captions: Keep your captions concise, engaging, and aligned with the tone and style of your brand. Use a hook or a question to capture attention and encourage users to watch your video. Consider adding relevant emojis to make your captions visually appealing.

b) Hashtags: Research and use relevant hashtags that are popular within your niche or related to the content of your video. Aim for a mix of broad and specific hashtags to increase the visibility of your videos. Analyze the performance of different hashtags and adjust your strategy accordingly.

c) Trending Hashtags: Keep an eye on trending hashtags and challenges on TikTok and incorporate them into your content when relevant. This can increase the chances of your videos being discovered by a wider audience.

d) Branded Hashtags: Create unique branded hashtags for your brand or specific campaigns. Encourage your audience to use these hashtags when creating content related to your brand, fostering a sense of community and increasing brand visibility.

3.3 Designing Engaging and Creative TikTok Videos

The heart of TikTok marketing lies in creating engaging and creative videos that captivate your audience. Here are some strategies to optimize your TikTok videos:

a) Storytelling: Use the power of storytelling to create narratives that resonate with your audience. Develop a clear beginning, middle, and end to keep viewers engaged throughout the video.

b) Visual Appeal: Pay attention to the visual elements of your videos, including lighting, composition, and colors. Experiment with different angles, camera movements, and video effects to add visual interest.

c) Music and Sound: Choose catchy music or audio tracks that complement the theme and mood of your video. TikTok provides a vast library of popular songs and sounds to enhance your content.

d) Editing Techniques: Utilize TikTok's built-in editing tools to add effects, filters, text overlays, and transitions to your videos. Experiment with different editing techniques to make your videos stand out.

e) Call-to-Action (CTA): Include a clear and compelling call-to-action in your videos to encourage users to engage with your content.

This could be liking the video, following your account, or visiting a specific link.

f) Video Length: While TikTok allows videos up to 60 seconds, consider keeping your videos shorter (15-30 seconds) for optimal engagement. Shorter videos tend to perform better and hold viewers' attention.

g) Engage with Trends: Keep up with the latest TikTok trends and challenges and participate in them when relevant to your brand. This helps your content stay fresh, relatable, and shareable.

By optimizing your TikTok profile, crafting attention-grabbing captions and hashtags, and designing engaging and creative videos, you'll be well on your way to maximizing your presence and impact on TikTok. In the next chapter, we'll explore strategies for growing your TikTok following and increasing engagement with your content.

Chapter 4

Understanding TikTok's Algorithm and Content Trends

4.1 Decoding the TikTok Algorithm and How it Works

To succeed on TikTok, it's crucial to understand the platform's algorithm and how it determines which content gets shown to users. While TikTok's algorithm is complex and constantly evolving, here are some key factors that influence its operation:

a) User Interactions: The algorithm takes into account how users interact with content. It considers factors such as likes, comments, shares, and saves. Videos that receive higher engagement are more likely to be recommended to a wider audience.

b) Video Completion Rate: TikTok values videos that keep users engaged till the end. The algorithm takes into account the percentage of viewers who watch the entire video. Creating compelling and captivating content can help improve your video completion rate.

c) Relevance and Interest: TikTok's algorithm aims to show users content that is relevant to their interests. It takes into account the type of content users engage with, the accounts they follow, and the hashtags they interact with. Tailoring your content to align with your target audience's interests can increase your chances of appearing in their feeds.

d) Video Details: The algorithm also considers video details such as captions, hashtags, and sounds. Using relevant and popular hashtags, crafting attention-grabbing captions, and leveraging trending sounds can boost the visibility of your content.

e) Device and Account Settings: The algorithm also takes into account factors like the user's device type and settings, language preference, and location. These factors can influence the content that appears in a user's feed.

Understanding these key factors can help you optimize your content strategy for TikTok and increase your chances of reaching a wider audience. However, it's important to note that TikTok's algorithm is dynamic, and it's essential to stay updated with any changes or updates that may occur.

4.2 Staying Updated with the Latest TikTok Trends and Challenges

TikTok thrives on trends and challenges that capture the attention of its user base. Staying updated with the latest trends and challenges is essential to keep your content relevant and engage with the TikTok community. Here are some strategies to stay in the loop:

a) Explore the Discover Page: The Discover page on TikTok is a treasure trove of trending content. Spend time regularly exploring this page to see what's currently popular and gaining traction. Take note of the types of videos, sounds, and hashtags that are trending.

b) Follow Trendsetters and Influencers: Follow popular TikTok creators and influencers in your niche to see what they're posting and which trends they're participating in. Pay attention to their content strategies, video styles, and engagement techniques.

c) Participate in Challenges: TikTok is known for its viral challenges. Participating in relevant challenges can boost your visibility and increase your chances of reaching a wider audience. Put your unique spin on the challenge to stand out and showcase your brand's personality.

d) Engage with Trending Sounds: TikTok has a vast library of trending sounds that can add an extra layer of appeal to your videos. Experiment with different sounds and incorporate them creatively into your content.

e) Monitor Popular Hashtags: Keep an eye on popular hashtags within your niche or industry. These hashtags can give you insights into the topics and themes that are currently trending on TikTok. Incorporate these hashtags into your content to increase discoverability.

f) Experiment and Innovate: While it's important to stay on top of trends, don't be afraid to experiment and innovate with your content. Creating unique and original videos can help you stand out from the crowd and attract attention from both TikTok users and the algorithm.

By staying updated with the latest TikTok trends and challenges, you can position yourself as a relevant and engaging creator. In the next section, we'll explore how you can leverage TikTok's Discovery page and For You page to maximize your content's visibility and reach.

Chapter 5

Growing Your TikTok Following and Engagement

5.1 Building an Authentic TikTok Community

Building an authentic TikTok community is essential for long-term success on the platform. Here are some strategies to help you foster a genuine and engaged following:

a) Consistency and Frequency: Consistency is key on TikTok. Regularly posting high-quality content can help you build a loyal following. Establish a posting schedule that works for you and stick to it.

Consistent posting keeps your audience engaged and signals to the TikTok algorithm that you're an active creator.

b) Authenticity and Transparency: TikTok users appreciate authenticity. Be yourself and showcase your brand's unique personality. Share behind-the-scenes moments, personal stories, and relatable content. Transparency builds trust with your audience and encourages them to engage with your content.

c) Respond to Comments and Messages: Engage with your audience by responding to comments and direct messages. Show appreciation for their support, answer their questions, and acknowledge their feedback. This level of interaction creates a sense of community and encourages others to engage with your content.

d) Collaborate with TikTok Creators: Collaborating with other TikTok creators can help you tap into their audience and expand your reach. Look for creators who align with your brand values and have a similar target audience. Collaborative content introduces your brand to new followers and creates opportunities for cross-promotion.

e) Encourage User-Generated Content (UGC): Encourage your followers to create and share content related to your brand. Host challenges or contests that prompt users to create videos featuring your products or brand message. User-generated content not only increases engagement but also serves as social proof, showcasing the positive experiences others have had with your brand.

5.2 Collaborating with TikTok Influencers and Creators

Collaborating with TikTok influencers and creators can significantly boost your brand's visibility and reach. Here's how to effectively collaborate with them:

a) Research and Identify Relevant Influencers: Look for influencers who have a genuine connection with your target audience and align with your brand values. Research their content, engagement rate, and audience demographics to ensure a good fit.

b) Reach Out and Negotiate: Contact influencers with a personalized message expressing your interest in collaborating. Discuss your campaign goals, budget, and expectations. Be open to negotiation and find mutually beneficial terms that align with both parties' objectives.

c) Specify Collaboration Requirements: Clearly communicate your expectations and the content you'd like the influencer to create. Provide them with any necessary guidelines, brand assets, or key messaging to ensure consistency and alignment with your brand.

d) Track and Measure Performance: Use tracking tools and analytics to measure the performance of influencer collaborations. Monitor key metrics such as reach, engagement, and conversions. This data will help you assess the effectiveness of the collaboration and inform future influencer partnerships.

5.3   Encouraging   User   Engagement   and Interaction

User engagement is crucial for TikTok success. Here are some effective strategies to encourage engagement with your TikTok content:

a) Pose Questions and Promote Discussions: Ask questions in your videos to spark conversations and encourage viewers to leave comments. Prompting viewers to share their opinions or experiences fosters engagement and creates a sense of community around your content.

b) Use Interactive Features: Leverage TikTok's interactive features such as polls, quizzes, and challenges. These features invite viewers to actively participate and engage with your content.

c) Run Contests and Giveaways: Hosting contests and giveaways is an excellent way to boost engagement. Encourage viewers to like, comment, and share your video for a chance to win a prize. This not only increases engagement but also helps spread awareness of your brand to a wider audience.

d) Respond and Engage with Comments: Make an effort to respond to comments on your TikTok videos. Engage in conversations, show appreciation for positive feedback, and address any questions or concerns. This level of interaction creates a positive user experience and encourages continued engagement.

e) Collaborate with Viewers: Invite viewers to participate in your videos by featuring their content or ideas. This collaboration not only increases engagement but also makes your audience feel valued and connected to your brand.

By implementing these strategies, you can effectively grow your TikTok following and foster a highly engaged community around your brand. Engagement is a key metric that signals to the TikTok algorithm that your content is valuable and relevant, leading to increased visibility and reach.

Chapter 6

Monetizing Your TikTok Presence

6.1 Exploring TikTok's Monetization Options and Opportunities

TikTok offers various monetization options and opportunities for content creators to generate revenue. Understanding these options can help you maximize your earning potential on the platform. Here are some key monetization avenues to explore:

a) TikTok Creator Fund: The TikTok Creator Fund allows eligible creators to earn money based on the performance of their content. Creators can apply to join the fund and, if accepted, receive regular payments based on factors such as video views, engagement, and region. Participating in the Creator Fund can provide a consistent income stream for your TikTok content.

b) Brand Partnerships and Sponsored Content: Collaborating with brands on sponsored content is a common way for TikTok creators to monetize their presence. Brands often seek out influencers and content creators with a significant following and engaged audience to promote their products or services. Negotiating brand partnerships and creating sponsored content can be a lucrative revenue stream for creators.

c) Affiliate Marketing: Affiliate marketing involves promoting products or services and earning a commission for each sale or lead generated through your referral. Many brands have affiliate programs that allow creators to earn a percentage of sales made through their unique affiliate links.

Integrating affiliate marketing into your TikTok content can be a passive income source.

d) Merchandise and E-commerce: If you have a dedicated fan base, consider launching your own merchandise or e-commerce store. This allows you to monetize your TikTok following by selling branded merchandise, products, or digital downloads. Engage with your audience to identify the types of products they would be interested in purchasing.

e) Livestreaming: TikTok's livestreaming feature provides an opportunity to earn virtual gifts from your viewers. Viewers can purchase virtual coins and send them as gifts during your livestream. These gifts can be converted into diamonds, which can then be exchanged for real money.

Livestreaming can be an interactive way to engage with your audience while monetizing your TikTok presence.

6.2 Creating Sponsored Content and Brand Partnerships

Sponsored content and brand partnerships are an effective way to monetize your TikTok presence. Here's how to create successful collaborations:

a) Authenticity and Alignment: When considering brand partnerships, choose brands that align with your content and resonate with your audience. Authenticity is crucial in maintaining your audience's trust, so only promote products or services that you genuinely believe in and that align with your values and niche.

b) Building Relationships: Establish relationships with brands by reaching out directly or through influencer marketing platforms. Highlight your TikTok analytics, engagement metrics, and the unique value you can bring to their campaign. Building a strong rapport with brands can lead to long-term partnerships and recurring sponsored opportunities.

c) Creating Compelling Sponsored Content: When creating sponsored content, ensure it blends seamlessly with your usual content style. Integrate the brand's message organically into your videos, keeping in mind your audience's preferences and expectations. Transparency is key, so clearly disclose when content is sponsored.

d) Negotiating Terms: When negotiating brand partnerships, consider factors such as deliverables, timeline, exclusivity, compensation, and rights usage. Be prepared to negotiate based on your reach, engagement, and the value you can provide to the brand. Ensure that the terms are mutually beneficial and align with your business goals.

e) Measuring Success: Track the performance of sponsored content using analytics tools provided by TikTok or third-party platforms. Monitor key metrics such as views, likes, comments, shares, and conversions. These insights will help you assess the success of your sponsored content and demonstrate value to future brand partners.

6.3 Maximizing Revenue with TikTok's Creator Fund and Livestreaming

In addition to sponsored content, TikTok provides two specific avenues for creators to maximize their revenue: the TikTok Creator Fund and livestreaming.

a) TikTok Creator Fund: The TikTok Creator Fund is a program that allows eligible creators to earn money based on their content's performance. To join the Creator Fund, creators must meet certain criteria set by TikTok, such as a minimum number of followers and views. Once accepted, creators receive regular payments based on their video views and engagement. Engaging with the Creator Fund can provide a consistent income stream for your TikTok presence.

b) Livestreaming and Virtual Gifts: TikTok's livestreaming feature enables you to interact with your audience in real-time. During livestreams, viewers can purchase virtual coins and send them as gifts to support you. These virtual gifts can be converted into diamonds, which can then be exchanged for real money. Livestreaming can be a fun and interactive way to engage with your audience while monetizing your TikTok presence.

c) Engaging Livestream Content: To maximize your livestream revenue, create engaging and interactive content that encourages viewers to participate. Plan special events, Q&A sessions, challenges, or exclusive content for your livestreams. Interact with your audience by responding to comments, acknowledging gifts, and giving shoutouts. Building a loyal and supportive community will increase the likelihood of receiving virtual gifts.

d) Promoting Your Livestreams: Prioritize promoting your livestreams to ensure maximum viewership. Utilize your TikTok feed, Stories, and other social media platforms to announce upcoming livestreams and share the schedule with your audience. Engage with your followers and encourage them to set reminders for your livestreams. Building anticipation and creating a sense of exclusivity can boost viewership and potential earnings.

By leveraging TikTok's monetization options, creating sponsored content, and maximizing revenue through the Creator Fund and livestreaming, you can turn your TikTok presence into a profitable venture while providing valuable content to your audience. Remember to maintain authenticity, prioritize audience engagement, and continually adapt your strategy to stay relevant in the dynamic world of TikTok.

Chapter 7

TikTok Analytics and Performance Tracking

7.1 Utilizing TikTok Analytics for Insights and Metrics

TikTok offers a robust analytics platform that provides valuable insights into your content's performance and audience engagement. Utilizing TikTok analytics is essential for gaining valuable insights and metrics about your content's performance on the platform. By understanding the data provided by TikTok, you can make informed decisions and optimize your TikTok marketing strategy.

Let's explore how you can effectively leverage TikTok analytics to drive your success on the platform.

1. Accessing TikTok Analytics:

To access TikTok analytics, you need to have a TikTok Pro account, which is free and available to all users. Once you've switched to a Pro account, you'll gain access to the analytics dashboard, where you can view various metrics and insights about your account and content.

2. Overview of TikTok Analytics Metrics:

TikTok analytics provides several key metrics that can help you gauge the performance of your content and understand your audience better.

Some of the essential metrics include:

a) Follower Insights: This metric provides you with an overview of your follower count, growth trends, and demographics. It gives you insights into the age range, gender distribution, and location of your followers. Understanding your audience demographics can help you tailor your content to their preferences and interests.

b) Content Insights: This metric focuses on the performance of your individual videos. You can view metrics such as views, likes, comments, shares, and engagement rates. Analyzing these metrics allows you to identify which videos resonate the most with your audience and replicate their success.

c) Profile Views: Profile view metrics help you understand how many users have visited your TikTok profile. By monitoring profile views, you can gauge the effectiveness of your profile optimization and the impact of your content on driving user curiosity to explore your account further.

d) Trending Content: TikTok analytics also highlights the content that is currently trending on your account. This feature allows you to identify which videos are gaining traction and resonating with your audience, providing valuable insights for future content creation.

3. Analyzing and Interpreting TikTok Analytics:

Once you have access to TikTok analytics and the metrics mentioned above, it's crucial to analyze and interpret the data effectively. Here are some tips for making the most of your analytics:

a) Identify Trends and Patterns: Look for patterns in your best-performing videos. Analyze the content, format, style, and topics that resonate with your audience the most. By identifying these trends, you can replicate successful elements in your future videos.

b) Audience Insights: Pay attention to the demographics of your audience. Understand their age, gender, and location to ensure your content aligns with their preferences. This information can help you tailor your content strategy and create content that appeals to your target audience.

c) Engagement Analysis: Dive deeper into engagement metrics such as likes, comments, shares, and video completion rates. Identify the content that generates the highest levels of engagement and interaction. This insight can guide you in creating more compelling and engaging videos.

d) Test and Experiment: Use TikTok analytics to measure the performance of different content formats, styles, and topics. Experiment with various approaches to understand what works best for your audience. By constantly testing and analyzing, you can refine your content strategy and optimize your TikTok presence.

4. Applying Insights to Your Strategy:

Once you've analyzed and interpreted the data from TikTok analytics, it's time to apply those insights to your TikTok marketing strategy. Here are some ways you can utilize the insights gained from TikTok analytics:

a) Content Optimization: Use the analytics data to optimize your content strategy. Create more of the content that performs well and resonates with your audience. Refine your content approach based on the topics, formats, and styles that generate higher engagement rates.

b) Audience Targeting: Leverage audience insights to refine your targeting strategy. Tailor your content to align with the demographics, preferences, and interests of your audience. This approach can help you build a loyal and engaged follower base.

c) Timing and Frequency: Analyze the data on when your content performs best. Identify the days and times when your audience is most active and adjust your posting schedule accordingly. Consistency and timing play a vital role in maximizing your reach and engagement.

d) Collaboration Opportunities: Utilize the insights from TikTok analytics to identify potential collaboration opportunities. Look for creators with similar target audiences and engagement levels. Collaborating with other TikTok creators can help you tap into their audience base and expand your reach.

5. Staying Updated with TikTok Changes:

TikTok is a dynamic platform, and its analytics features may evolve over time. Stay updated with any changes or additions to the analytics dashboard. Follow official TikTok announcements, join relevant communities, and engage with TikTok marketing resources to ensure you are leveraging the most up-to-date analytics tools.

TikTok analytics provides valuable insights and metrics that can help you understand your audience, optimize your content, and refine your TikTok marketing strategy. By analyzing the data, applying the insights gained, and staying informed about platform changes, you can enhance your performance on TikTok, drive engagement, and grow your presence on the platform.

7.2 Tracking Video Performance and Audience Engagement

Monitoring your video performance and audience engagement is crucial for optimizing your TikTok strategy.

Tracking video performance and audience engagement is crucial for understanding the effectiveness of your TikTok marketing efforts. By monitoring key metrics and analyzing audience behavior, you can make data-driven decisions to optimize your content and increase engagement. In this section, we will explore the importance of tracking video performance and audience engagement on TikTok and discuss the key metrics to consider.

1. Why Tracking Video Performance and Audience Engagement Matters:

Tracking video performance and audience engagement allows you to assess the impact and effectiveness of your TikTok content. It provides valuable insights into how users interact with your videos, which helps you understand what resonates with your audience and what doesn't. By monitoring these metrics, you can identify areas for improvement, refine your content strategy, and ultimately drive better results.

2. Key Metrics for Tracking Video Performance and Engagement:

a) Views: The number of views indicates how many times your video has been seen by TikTok users. Tracking views helps you understand the reach of your content and its potential to go viral.

b) Likes: Likes represent the number of users who have expressed their appreciation for your video by tapping the heart button. Monitoring likes can give you an idea of how well your content is received by your audience.

c) Comments: Comments reflect the level of engagement and interaction your video generates. Pay attention to the type of comments you receive, as they can provide valuable feedback and insights from your audience.

d) Shares: Shares indicate the number of times users have shared your video with others. A high share count suggests that your content resonates with viewers and has the potential to reach a wider audience.

e) Saves: Saves represent the number of times users have saved your video to their "Favorites" or collections. This metric shows that your content is valuable or interesting enough for users to want to revisit it later.

f) Video Completion Rate: The video completion rate reveals the percentage of viewers who watch your entire video. A higher completion rate indicates that your content is compelling and engaging, keeping users hooked until the end.

g) Engagement Rate: The engagement rate measures the level of interaction on your video, taking into account likes, comments, shares, and saves. It provides an overall assessment of how well your video resonates with your audience.

h) Click-through Rate (CTR): CTR measures the percentage of viewers who click on your profile or take a specific action after watching your video. It helps evaluate the effectiveness of your call-to-action (CTA) or your ability to drive traffic to your website or other platforms.

3. Monitoring and Analyzing Metrics:

To effectively track video performance and audience engagement, it's important to consistently monitor these metrics and analyze the data. Here are some strategies to help you make the most of the data:

a) Regularly Check Insights: TikTok provides insights and analytics for each of your videos. Take the time to review these insights and identify trends or patterns in the performance metrics.

b) Compare Performance: Compare the performance of different videos to understand what type of content performs best. Identify common elements or themes that drive higher engagement and replicate those strategies in future videos.

c) Analyze Audience Behavior: Look for patterns in audience behavior, such as peak engagement times or popular video formats. This information can help you optimize your posting schedule and tailor your content to better align with your audience's preferences.

d) Listen to Feedback: Pay attention to comments and messages from your audience. They may provide valuable insights or suggestions for future content. Engage with your audience by responding to comments and fostering a sense of community.

e) Experiment and Iterate: Use the data from video performance and audience engagement to guide your content experimentation. Try different formats, styles, and topics to see what resonates best with your audience. Continuously refine your strategy based on the insights gained.

4. Tools for Tracking

Video Performance and Engagement:

TikTok provides its own analytics dashboard, which offers insights into video performance and audience engagement. Additionally, you can leverage third-party social media analytics tools that provide more in-depth data and analysis. Some popular tools for tracking TikTok metrics include Socialbakers, Influencer Marketing Hub, and Sprout Social.

5. Actionable Insights from Video Performance and Engagement Data:

By analyzing the data on video performance and audience engagement, you can derive actionable insights to improve your TikTok marketing strategy. Here are some examples:

a) Identify Trending Topics: Analyze the performance of videos related to specific topics or trends. This can help you identify popular content themes to incorporate into your strategy.

b) Optimize Video Length: Determine the ideal video length for your target audience by assessing the video completion rate. Experiment with different video lengths and monitor engagement to find the sweet spot.

c) Refine Content Strategy: Use the data to refine your content strategy. Focus on creating videos that generate high engagement and replicate successful content formats.

d) Tailor Your Approach: Analyze audience demographics and engagement patterns to better understand your target audience. Tailor your content, tone, and approach to align with their preferences and interests.

e) Collaborate with Influencers: Identify influencers who have a similar target audience and analyze their video performance and engagement. Consider collaborating with them to expand your reach and engage with a wider audience.

In conclusion, tracking video performance and audience engagement on TikTok is essential for optimizing your content strategy and achieving marketing success. By monitoring key metrics, analyzing the data, and implementing actionable insights, you can refine your approach, create more engaging content, and build a strong TikTok presence. Remember, continuous monitoring and adaptation are key to staying ahead in the ever-evolving landscape of TikTok.

7.3 Optimizing Your TikTok Strategy Based on Data

Analyzing TikTok analytics and performance metrics allows you to make informed decisions to optimize your TikTok strategy. Here are some strategies to consider:

a) Identify Top-Performing Content: Review the analytics of your top-performing videos to identify common themes, formats, or trends that resonate with your audience. Use this information to inform your content creation and replicate the success of those videos.

b) Experiment with Different Content Formats: TikTok offers a variety of content formats, including duets, challenges, and trends. Analyze the performance of different content formats to understand what type of content generates the most engagement from your audience. Experimenting with different formats keeps your content fresh and encourages audience participation.

c) Refine Your Posting Schedule: Analyze your content performance based on the time and day of posting. Identify patterns in audience engagement and adjust your posting schedule accordingly. Posting at times when your audience is most active can help maximize your reach and engagement.

d) Engage with Your Audience: Responding to comments, engaging in conversations, and acknowledging your audience's feedback helps foster a sense of community and strengthens your relationship with your followers. Encourage audience participation and actively engage with your viewers to build loyalty and increase overall engagement.

e) Monitor Trending Content: Stay updated with the latest TikTok trends and challenges. Incorporate relevant trends into your content strategy to tap into the existing buzz and reach a wider audience. Monitoring trending content allows you to stay relevant and adapt your content to align with the interests of your audience.

By utilizing TikTok analytics and tracking your content's performance and audience engagement, you can gain valuable insights into your TikTok strategy's effectiveness. Use this data to optimize your content, refine your posting schedule, and engage with your audience to drive continuous growth and maximize your impact on TikTok.

Chapter 8

TikTok Advertising and Paid Promotions

8.1 Introduction to TikTok Ads and Ad Formats

TikTok Ads offer a powerful opportunity for businesses and marketers to reach a vast and engaged audience on the platform. With its growing popularity and diverse user base, TikTok has become an attractive advertising platform for brands looking to connect with their target customers. In this chapter, we will provide an introduction to TikTok Ads and explore the various ad formats available to advertisers.

1. What are TikTok Ads?

TikTok Ads are paid advertising placements that allow businesses to promote their products, services, or brand on the TikTok platform. These ads appear in users' feeds, and they blend seamlessly with organic content, providing an immersive and engaging advertising experience. TikTok offers a range of ad formats to suit different campaign goals and creative strategies.

2. Benefits of TikTok Ads:

a) Wide Reach: With over a billion monthly active users, TikTok offers a massive reach and the potential to connect with a global audience. This is especially beneficial for businesses aiming to expand their brand awareness or tap into new markets.

b) Engaged User Base: TikTok users are highly engaged, spending an average of several hours on the app each day. This level of engagement presents a unique opportunity for brands to capture the attention of their target audience and drive meaningful interactions.

c) Creativity and Authenticity: TikTok's emphasis on creative and authentic content aligns well with advertising campaigns that prioritize storytelling and engaging visuals. Brands can leverage TikTok's creative tools and formats to create compelling and memorable ads that resonate with users.

d) Targeting Capabilities: TikTok provides robust targeting options to ensure that ads reach the right audience. Advertisers can define their target audience based on factors such as demographics, interests, location, and behavior, allowing for precise audience segmentation.

3. TikTok Ad Formats:

TikTok offers a variety of ad formats to cater to different marketing goals and creative strategies. Let's explore some of the most popular ad formats available on the platform:

a) In-Feed Ads: In-Feed Ads appear in users' TikTok feeds as they scroll through the app.

These ads can include images, videos, and clickable links. In-Feed Ads allow businesses to create immersive, full-screen experiences and capture users' attention with engaging visuals and compelling messaging.

b) Brand Takeover: Brand Takeover ads are full-screen ads that appear when users open the TikTok app. These ads provide an immediate and impactful brand presence, making them effective for driving brand awareness and delivering a specific message to users upon app launch.

c) TopView: TopView ads are similar to Brand Takeover ads but offer more extended exposure. They are the first ad users see when they open the TikTok app and can last up to 60 seconds. TopView ads enable businesses to create captivating stories or showcase product demonstrations.

d) Branded Hashtag Challenges: Branded Hashtag Challenges encourage users to participate in a brand-specific challenge and create their content around it. These challenges can generate user-generated content and virality, enabling brands to amplify their reach and engagement.

e) Branded Effects: Branded Effects are augmented reality (AR) filters and effects that users can apply to their videos. Brands can create their customized filters to promote their products or enhance brand recognition through user-generated content.

4. Getting Started with TikTok Ads:

To get started with TikTok Ads, follow these steps:

a) Create an Ad Account: Sign up for a TikTok Ads account and complete the necessary registration process.

b) Set Campaign Objectives: Define your campaign goals, such as brand awareness, website traffic, or app installs. TikTok Ads offers various objective options to align with your marketing objectives.

c) Target Your Audience: Specify your target audience based on demographics, interests, location, and other relevant criteria.

d) Choose Ad Formats: Select the ad formats that best suit your campaign goals and creative strategy.

e) Set Budget and Schedule: Determine your advertising budget and schedule your campaign based on your marketing objectives and available resources.

f) Monitor and Optimize: Continuously monitor the performance of your ads, make necessary adjustments, and optimize your campaigns for better results.

In conclusion, TikTok Ads provide businesses with a unique opportunity to reach a vast and engaged audience. By leveraging the platform's diverse ad formats, targeting capabilities, and creative tools, advertisers can create compelling and immersive advertising experiences that resonate with TikTok users. Whether you aim to drive brand awareness, increase website traffic, or promote specific products, TikTok Ads can be a valuable addition to your digital marketing strategy.

8.2 Setting Up and Managing Effective TikTok Ad Campaigns

Setting up and managing effective TikTok ad campaigns requires careful planning, strategic execution, and continuous optimization. In this section, we will discuss the essential steps and best practices for setting up and managing TikTok ad campaigns that deliver impactful results.

1. Define Your Campaign Objectives:

Before diving into setting up your TikTok ad campaign, it's crucial to define your campaign objectives. What do you want to achieve with your ads? Is it brand awareness, lead generation, app installs, or sales? Clearly defining your objectives will guide your campaign strategy and help you measure success.

2. Understand Your Target Audience:

Understanding your target audience is key to creating ads that resonate with them. Conduct thorough research to identify the demographics, interests, behaviors, and preferences of your target audience on TikTok. This information will help you tailor your ad messaging, visuals, and targeting options to reach the right users.

3. Choose the Right Ad Format:

TikTok offers a range of ad formats, each suited for different campaign goals. Consider the nature of your business and campaign objectives to select the most appropriate ad format. Whether it's In-Feed Ads, Brand Takeover, TopView, Branded Hashtag Challenges, or Branded Effects, choose the format that aligns with your goals and engages your target audience effectively.

4. Craft Compelling Ad Creative:

Creating visually appealing and engaging ad creative is essential for capturing users' attention on TikTok. Leverage the platform's creative tools, such as filters, effects, and music, to enhance your ad content. Experiment with different video lengths, styles, and storytelling techniques to make your ads stand out. Remember to align your creative with your brand identity and campaign objectives.

5. Implement Effective Targeting:

TikTok provides several targeting options to ensure your ads reach the right audience. Use demographic filters such as age, gender, and location to narrow down your target audience. Additionally, take advantage of interest-based targeting, which allows you to target users who have shown an interest in specific topics related to your business. Experiment with different targeting options to refine your audience reach and maximize campaign effectiveness.

6. Set Budget and Bidding Strategy:

Determine your advertising budget and allocate it wisely across your TikTok ad campaigns. Consider factors such as campaign duration, ad formats, and audience reach when setting your budget. TikTok offers various bidding strategies, including Cost Per Impression (CPM) and Cost Per Click (CPC). Choose the bidding strategy that aligns with your campaign objectives and monitor its performance to optimize results.

7. Monitor and Optimize Campaign Performance:

Continuous monitoring and optimization are essential for ensuring the success of your TikTok ad campaigns. Track key performance metrics such as impressions, clicks, click-through rates, conversions, and return on ad spend (ROAS). Identify areas of improvement and make data-driven adjustments to your targeting, creative, and bidding strategies.

8. A/B Testing:

To maximize the effectiveness of your TikTok ad campaigns, conduct A/B testing. Test different variations of your ad creative, messaging, targeting options, and bidding strategies to identify the most effective combinations. Analyze the results and optimize your campaigns based on the insights gained from the testing process.

9. Leverage TikTok Pixel:

TikTok Pixel is a tracking tool that allows you to measure the effectiveness of your ad campaigns, optimize conversions, and create remarketing audiences. Implement the TikTok Pixel on your website or app to gain valuable insights into user behavior and retarget users who have shown interest in your brand.

10. Regularly Review and Refine Your Strategy:

TikTok's ad landscape is constantly evolving, and user preferences can change over time. It's crucial to regularly review your ad campaigns, analyze performance data, and refine your strategy accordingly. Stay updated with new features, ad formats, and targeting options that TikTok introduces to leverage the platform's full potential.

By following these steps and best practices, you can set up and manage effective TikTok ad campaigns that deliver impactful results.

Remember to continuously monitor, optimize, and refine your strategies to ensure your ads resonate with your target audience and drive the desired outcomes.

8.3 Targeting Specific Audiences and Analyzing Ad Performance

To target specific audiences and analyze ad performance on TikTok, follow these steps:

a) Audience Targeting: Utilize TikTok's targeting options to narrow down your audience based on demographics, interests, and behaviors. Refine your targeting based on audience insights and optimize your campaigns to reach the most relevant users.

b) Tracking and Conversion Pixels: Implement TikTok's tracking and conversion pixels on your website or app to measure the effectiveness of your ad campaigns. Conversion pixels allow you

to track key actions taken by users, such as purchases or form submissions, providing valuable data for campaign optimization.

c) Ad Performance Analysis: Regularly monitor and analyze the performance of your TikTok ads. Review metrics like impressions, click-through rates, engagement rates, and conversion rates to assess the effectiveness of your campaigns. Identify top-performing ads and optimize underperforming ones to improve overall campaign performance.

d) A/B Testing: Conduct A/B testing to compare different ad variations and optimize your campaigns further. Test different creative elements, ad formats, targeting options, and ad copies to identify the most effective combinations. Use the insights gained from A/B testing to refine your ad campaigns and maximize results.

e) Ongoing Campaign Optimization: Continuously optimize your TikTok ad campaigns based on data-driven insights and performance analysis. Make adjustments to targeting, creative elements, and bidding strategies to improve ad relevance, engagement, and overall return on investment.

By understanding TikTok's advertising options, setting up effective ad campaigns, and targeting specific audiences, you can leverage TikTok's vast user base to drive engagement and achieve your marketing goals. Regularly analyze ad performance, make data-driven optimizations, and refine your strategies to maximize the impact of your TikTok advertising efforts.

Chapter 9

TikTok Success Stories and Case Studies

9.1 Inspiring Examples of Brands and Individuals that Mastered TikTok Marketing

TikTok has become a breeding ground for creativity and viral content, providing countless opportunities for brands and individuals to showcase their talents, products, and messages. In this chapter, we will explore inspiring examples of brands and individuals that have mastered TikTok marketing and achieved remarkable success. These success stories will serve as a source of inspiration and valuable insights for your own TikTok marketing efforts.

a) Brand Success Stories: Discover how well-known brands have utilized TikTok to engage with their target audience and drive brand awareness. From established companies to emerging startups, learn about their creative approaches, innovative campaigns, and the impact they made on the platform. These success stories will showcase how brands leveraged TikTok's features, user-generated content, and influencer collaborations to create memorable experiences and build strong brand communities.

b) Individual Success Stories: TikTok is not only a platform for brands but also a platform for individuals to express their creativity, showcase their talents, and gain a massive following. Explore the stories of TikTok creators who have risen to fame through their engaging and entertaining content. Learn about their journey, the strategies they employed, and the lessons they have learned along the way. These stories will demonstrate the power of authenticity, consistency, and connecting with the TikTok community.

9.2 Learning from Successful TikTok Campaigns and Strategies

Successful TikTok campaigns require a deep understanding of the platform, its audience, and the creative trends that resonate with users. In this section, we will delve into specific TikTok campaigns that have generated significant traction and engagement. By analyzing these campaigns, you will gain valuable insights into the key elements that contribute to their success.

a) Creative Content Strategies: Examine the content strategies employed by successful TikTok campaigns. Understand how they leveraged TikTok's unique features, such as music, effects, and duets, to create compelling and shareable content. Explore the storytelling techniques, humor, and authenticity that made these campaigns stand out and capture the attention of TikTok users.

b) Influencer Collaborations: Influencers play a vital role in TikTok marketing, as they have the ability to reach and engage with a vast audience. Learn how brands strategically collaborated with influencers to amplify their message, increase brand visibility, and drive user-generated content. Discover the best practices for identifying and partnering with the right influencers on TikTok to ensure the success of your campaigns.

c) User-Generated Content Campaigns: TikTok thrives on user-generated content, and brands have found innovative ways to tap into this trend. Explore successful user-generated content campaigns on TikTok and learn how brands encouraged their audience to participate, create their own content, and become brand advocates. Discover the techniques for launching effective challenges, contests, and hashtag campaigns to inspire and engage TikTok users.

9.3 Analyzing Different Approaches for Various Goals

Every brand and individual on TikTok has unique goals and objectives. In this section, we will analyze different approaches taken by brands and individuals based on their specific goals. Whether your aim is to increase brand awareness, drive sales, or foster community engagement, understanding the strategies employed by others will help you tailor your own TikTok marketing approach.

a) Brand Awareness and Reach: Explore how brands have used TikTok to build brand awareness and reach new audiences. Discover the tactics for creating viral content, leveraging popular TikTok trends, and collaborating with influencers to maximize exposure. Learn how to create a memorable brand presence on TikTok that resonates with users and encourages them to share and engage with your content.

b) Driving Sales and Conversions: TikTok offers opportunities for brands to drive sales and conversions by showcasing products, running promotions, and driving traffic

to e-commerce platforms. Analyze successful TikTok campaigns that effectively converted viewers into customers. Learn about strategies for incorporating product placements, call-to-action buttons, and shoppable features to drive conversions and measure the return on investment.

c) Community Engagement and Advocacy: TikTok is not just about creating content; it's about building a community and fostering engagement. Explore how brands have successfully built a loyal and engaged community on TikTok through interactive content, meaningful conversations, and user participation. Understand the strategies for nurturing brand advocates, encouraging user-generated content, and fostering a sense of belonging within the TikTok community.

By studying these TikTok success stories and case studies, you will gain valuable insights into the strategies, tactics, and creative approaches that have proven effective on the platform. Use these examples as inspiration to develop your own unique TikTok marketing strategies and campaigns, tailored to your brand's goals and target audience.

Chapter 10

Future Trends in TikTok Marketing

TikTok is a dynamic and ever-evolving platform, constantly introducing new features, formats, and trends. In this chapter, we will explore the future trends in TikTok marketing and discuss how brands and individuals can stay ahead of the curve to maximize their success on the platform.

10.1 Embracing New Features and Formats on TikTok

TikTok is known for its innovative features and formats that keep users engaged and entertained. As a TikTok marketer, it's crucial to stay updated with the latest features and embrace them in your marketing strategies. In this section, we will explore upcoming features and formats that are expected to make an impact on TikTok marketing.

a) Augmented Reality (AR) Effects: TikTok is continuously expanding its library of AR effects, allowing users to enhance their videos with filters, masks, and interactive elements. Discover how brands can leverage AR effects to create immersive and interactive experiences for their audience. Explore the possibilities of incorporating branded AR effects to drive engagement and brand recall.

b) TikTok LIVE: Live streaming is gaining popularity on TikTok, enabling users to connect with their audience in real-time. Learn how brands can leverage TikTok LIVE to host interactive sessions, product launches, Q&A sessions, and behind-the-scenes experiences. Explore the potential of live shopping experiences and collaborations with influencers to drive sales and engagement.

c) TikTok Shorts: Shorts are short-form vertical videos similar to TikTok's rival platform, YouTube Shorts. Understand how TikTok Shorts can be used as a standalone feature or as a cross-platform promotion tool. Explore the strategies for creating engaging Shorts content and leveraging the Shorts algorithm to reach a wider audience.

10.2 Exploring Cross-Platform Integration and Collaboration

TikTok's influence extends beyond its own platform, and cross-platform integration and collaboration have become essential for successful TikTok marketing. In this section, we will discuss the importance of integrating TikTok with other social media platforms and explore opportunities for collaboration.

a) Cross-Platform Promotion: Understand the strategies for promoting your TikTok content on other social media platforms, such as Instagram, Twitter, and YouTube. Learn how to create teaser content, behind-the-scenes footage, and exclusive content to drive traffic to your TikTok profile and increase your follower base.

b) Influencer Collaborations: Influencer marketing continues to be a powerful tool on TikTok. Explore how brands can collaborate with influencers across multiple platforms to amplify their message and reach a wider audience. Understand the strategies for identifying the right influencers, negotiating partnerships, and creating compelling content that resonates with their audience.

c) Brand Partnerships: TikTok has become a platform for brand collaborations and partnerships. Discover the opportunities for cross-platform brand partnerships, where brands can collaborate with other brands or content creators to create engaging and shareable content. Explore the strategies for identifying suitable partners, aligning brand values, and executing successful collaborations that benefit both parties.

10.3 *Staying Ahead in the Dynamic World of TikTok Marketing*

TikTok's fast-paced and dynamic nature requires marketers to be agile and adaptive. In this section, we will discuss strategies for staying ahead in the world of TikTok marketing and keeping up with the platform's evolving trends.

a) Monitoring TikTok Trends: TikTok is known for its viral trends and challenges. Stay updated with the latest TikTok trends by monitoring the Discover page, following relevant hashtags, and engaging with the TikTok community. Understand how to incorporate these trends into your content strategy to increase visibility and engagement.

b) Data-driven Decision Making: As TikTok provides insights and analytics, leverage this data to make informed decisions about your content strategy. Analyze metrics such as views, likes, shares, and comments to understand what resonates with your audience. Use this data to optimize your content, experiment with new ideas, and refine your TikTok marketing approach.

c) Continuous Learning and Experimentation: TikTok is a platform that rewards creativity and experimentation. Encourage a culture of continuous learning within your team and be open to trying new ideas and formats. Embrace a test-and-learn approach, where you constantly analyze the performance of your content and make adjustments based on audience feedback.

By embracing new features and formats, exploring cross-platform integration and collaboration, and staying ahead of the trends, you can position your brand for long-term success on TikTok. The dynamic nature of the platform offers endless possibilities for creative expression and audience engagement, making it an exciting platform for marketers to explore and leverage in their marketing strategies.

Chapter 11: Navigating Challenges and Overcoming Obstacles on TikTok

11.1 Understanding Common Challenges on TikTok

TikTok has rapidly grown in popularity and has become a highly influential platform for marketers and content creators. However, like any social media platform, TikTok presents its own set of challenges and obstacles that marketers must navigate to maximize their success. In this section, we will explore some of the common challenges faced on TikTok and discuss strategies to overcome them.

1. Fluctuations in Reach and Engagement:

One of the most common challenges on TikTok is dealing with fluctuations in reach and engagement. TikTok's algorithm is constantly evolving, and changes in the algorithm can impact the visibility of your content. You may experience periods of high engagement and reach, followed by periods of lower visibility. To overcome this challenge, it's crucial to stay informed about any algorithm updates and adapt your content strategy accordingly. Keep an eye on trending content and user preferences, and adjust your approach to ensure that your content remains relevant and engaging.

2. Content Saturation:

TikTok is a highly competitive platform, with millions of users creating and sharing content every day. This saturation of content can make it challenging to stand out and capture the attention of your target audience. To overcome this challenge, it's important to focus on creating unique and high-quality content that sets you apart from the competition. Identify your niche and explore innovative ways to present your content. Leveraging popular trends and challenges can also help increase your visibility and attract new followers.

3. Maintaining Consistency:

Consistency is key on TikTok, as it helps build trust and engagement with your audience. However, consistently creating and publishing content can be a challenge, especially if you have limited time or resources. To overcome this challenge, it's essential to develop a content strategy and create a content calendar. Plan your content in advance and allocate dedicated time for content creation and scheduling. This will ensure a consistent flow of content and help you stay on top of your TikTok game.

4. Balancing Authenticity and Promotion:

TikTok users value authenticity, and finding the right balance between promoting your brand and being authentic can be a challenge. Blatantly promotional content may not resonate well with the TikTok community, and it's important to approach promotional content in a creative and authentic way. Instead of solely focusing on sales pitches, aim to create content that provides value, entertains, or educates your audience. Infuse your brand personality into your content and make genuine connections with your followers.

5. Handling Negative Comments and Feedback:

As your TikTok following grows, you may encounter negative comments or feedback from users. Dealing with negativity can be emotionally challenging, but it's important to address these situations in a constructive and professional manner. Avoid engaging in arguments or responding defensively. Instead, focus on fostering a positive and supportive community by replying politely and addressing concerns respectfully. Encourage constructive feedback and use it as an opportunity to learn and improve your content.

6. Copyright and Intellectual Property Issues:

TikTok is a platform where users can create and share content, which can sometimes raise concerns about copyright and intellectual property infringement. It's crucial to understand the platform's guidelines and policies regarding copyrighted material and ensure that you respect the rights of others. Avoid using copyrighted music or content without proper permission, and be cautious when creating content inspired by others. Protect your own intellectual property by watermarking your original content and monitoring for unauthorized use.

7. Staying Relevant and Embracing TikTok Trends:

TikTok is known for its viral trends and challenges, and staying relevant can be a challenge in itself. To overcome this challenge, actively participate in trending challenges and incorporate popular hashtags into your content strategy. Stay up to date with the latest TikTok trends by regularly exploring the "Discover" and

"For You" pages. Adapt your content to align with the current trends, while still maintaining your brand identity and values.

Understanding and proactively addressing the common challenges on TikTok is essential for marketers and content creators to succeed on the platform.

By staying informed about algorithm updates, creating unique and high-quality content, maintaining consistency, balancing authenticity and promotion, handling negativity professionally, respecting copyright and intellectual property, and staying relevant with TikTok trends, you can navigate these challenges and enhance your TikTok marketing efforts.

Remember, challenges are opportunities for growth, and with the right strategies in place, you can overcome any obstacle and thrive on TikTok.

11.2 Dealing with Algorithm Changes

TikTok's algorithm plays a crucial role in determining the visibility and reach of your content on the platform. It constantly evolves to provide users with a personalized and engaging experience. However, these algorithm changes can sometimes result in fluctuations in reach and engagement, presenting a challenge for marketers and content creators. In this section, we will discuss strategies to navigate algorithm changes and maintain consistent performance on TikTok.

1. Stay Informed and Adapt Quickly:

To effectively deal with algorithm changes, it's crucial to stay informed about updates and modifications to TikTok's algorithm. Follow official TikTok channels, join relevant communities, and keep an eye on industry news and updates. TikTok often announces algorithm changes or provides guidelines to help creators understand the new algorithms. By staying informed, you can adapt your content strategy quickly and make necessary adjustments to align with the updated algorithm.

2. Focus on Quality and Engagement:

The TikTok algorithm prioritizes content that is engaging, retains viewer attention, and receives positive feedback. Regardless of algorithm changes, focusing on creating high-quality and engaging content should always be a priority. Produce content that resonates with your target audience, encourages interaction, and prompts viewers to share and engage with your content. By consistently delivering valuable and entertaining content, you can maintain strong engagement levels even during algorithm changes.

3. Analyze Your Performance Metrics:

Monitoring and analyzing your TikTok performance metrics is essential to understand how algorithm changes impact your content's reach and engagement. Pay close attention to metrics such as views, likes, shares, comments, and audience retention rates. By analyzing these metrics, you can identify patterns, trends, and changes in your content's performance. This insight will help you understand how algorithm changes affect your content and enable you to make data-driven decisions to optimize your strategy accordingly.

4. Embrace Trending Content and Challenges:

TikTok's algorithm heavily promotes trending content and challenges. During algorithm changes, it's beneficial to leverage these trends to maintain visibility and engagement. Participate in popular challenges, incorporate relevant hashtags, and create content that aligns with the current trends. This proactive approach can help your content gain traction and increase its chances of appearing on the "For You" page, where it can reach a wider audience.

5. Diversify Your Content Strategy:

Algorithm changes can be an opportunity to diversify your content strategy and experiment with different formats, styles, and topics. By diversifying your content, you can cater to a broader range of interests and preferences, increasing the likelihood of resonating with different segments of the TikTok audience. Try incorporating various types of content, such as educational videos, behind-the-scenes glimpses, challenges, or storytelling. Keep a close eye on how different types of content perform and adjust your strategy accordingly.

6. Engage with Your Audience:

Building a strong and engaged community on TikTok is essential for long-term success. During algorithm changes, prioritize engaging with your audience through comments, replies, and direct messages. Encourage discussions, ask questions, and respond to user-generated content related to your brand. By fostering meaningful connections with your audience, you can maintain strong engagement levels, which can positively impact your content's visibility on the platform.

7. Collaborate with Influencers:

Influencer collaborations can be a powerful strategy to overcome algorithm changes and expand your reach on TikTok. Collaborating with influencers who have a relevant audience can help expose your brand to a wider user base and increase your content's visibility. Partner with influencers whose values align with your brand and develop creative campaigns that resonate with their followers. By leveraging the influencer's existing reach and engagement, you can navigate algorithm changes more effectively.

Algorithm changes are a natural part of any social media platform's evolution, and TikTok is no exception. By staying informed, focusing on quality and engagement, analyzing performance metrics, embracing trends, diversifying your content strategy, engaging with your audience, and collaborating with influencers, you can navigate algorithm changes effectively and maintain consistent performance on TikTok. Remember that building a strong and authentic presence takes time and effort, so stay persistent, adapt to changes, and continue to create valuable content that resonates with your target audience.

11.3 Handling Negative Comments and Feedback

As your TikTok presence grows, you may encounter negative comments or feedback from users. It's essential to have strategies in place to handle such situations in a constructive manner. We will explore ways to address negative comments, turn criticism into opportunities, and maintain a positive and respectful online environment.

11.4 Managing Copyright and Intellectual Property Issues

TikTok is a platform where users can create and share content, which sometimes raises concerns about copyright and intellectual property. It's crucial to understand the platform's guidelines and policies regarding copyrighted material and to ensure that you respect the rights of others. We will discuss best practices for avoiding copyright infringement and protecting your own intellectual property on TikTok.

11.5 Maintaining Consistency and Momentum

Consistency is key on TikTok, as it helps build trust and engagement with your audience. However, it can be challenging to consistently create and publish content while also maintaining quality and relevance. We will provide strategies for managing your TikTok content calendar, planning ahead, and staying consistent in your content production.

11.6 Overcoming Creative Blocks

Creativity plays a significant role in TikTok marketing, but creative blocks can happen to anyone. When faced with a creative block, it's important to have techniques and strategies to overcome it and generate fresh ideas. We will explore methods to spark creativity, overcome creative blocks, and maintain a steady stream of engaging content on TikTok.

11.7 Building Resilience and Long-Term Success

TikTok marketing is not an overnight success; it requires patience, persistence, and resilience. Building a strong TikTok presence takes time and effort, and setbacks are a part of the journey. We will discuss strategies for maintaining motivation, learning from setbacks, and fostering long-term success on TikTok.

11.8 Embracing TikTok Trends and Staying Relevant

TikTok is known for its viral trends and challenges, and staying up to date with the latest trends can be a challenge in itself. We will explore ways to embrace TikTok trends, participate in challenges, and stay relevant in a rapidly evolving TikTok landscape.

11.9 Balancing Authenticity and Promotion

Authenticity is highly valued on TikTok, and striking the right balance between promoting your brand and being authentic can be a delicate task. We will discuss strategies for maintaining authenticity while incorporating promotional content effectively on TikTok.

In this chapter, we have addressed the common challenges and obstacles that marketers and content creators may face on TikTok. By understanding and proactively navigating these challenges, you can enhance your TikTok marketing efforts and achieve long-term success on the platform. Remember, challenges are opportunities for growth, and with the right strategies in place, you can overcome any obstacle and thrive on TikTok.

Appendix

Helpful Tools for TikTok Marketing

In this appendix, we will explore a range of useful tools and resources that can enhance your TikTok marketing efforts. These tools are designed to streamline your workflow, optimize your content, and provide valuable insights to help you achieve success on TikTok.

1. TikTok Analytics and Insights Tools

   - TikTok Pro: TikTok's built-in analytics tool that provides valuable insights about your account's performance, follower demographics, and trending videos.

   - Influencer Marketing Platforms: Platforms like CreatorIQ, Upfluence, and NeoReach that help you find and connect with TikTok influencers for brand collaborations and influencer marketing campaigns.

2. Video Editing Software and Apps

   - Adobe Premiere Pro: A professional-grade video editing software that offers advanced editing features and allows you to create high-quality TikTok videos.

   - InShot: A user-friendly mobile video editing app that enables you to trim, merge, add effects, and customize your TikTok videos on the go.

   - CapCut: A popular video editing app with a wide range of editing tools, effects, and filters to enhance your TikTok videos.

3. Hashtag Research Tools

   - TikTok's Discover Page: Explore the trending hashtags and challenges on TikTok's Discover Page to gain inspiration and identify popular trends.

   - Hashtagify: A hashtag research tool that helps you find relevant and trending hashtags for your TikTok content.

4. TikTok Growth and Management Tools

- TokUpgrade: A TikTok growth service that helps you increase your follower count and engagement through targeted audience interactions.

- Later: A social media scheduling tool that allows you to plan and schedule your TikTok content in advance, ensuring consistent posting.

5. TikTok Advertising and Analytics Platforms

- TikTok Ads Manager: TikTok's advertising platform that enables you to create, manage, and track your TikTok ad campaigns.

- SocialPeta: An advertising intelligence tool that provides insights and data on successful TikTok ad campaigns, helping you optimize your ad strategy.

6. Music and Sound Libraries

- TikTok Sounds: Explore TikTok's extensive library of music and sounds to find catchy tunes and audio clips that align with your content.

- Epidemic Sound: A royalty-free music platform that offers a vast collection of high-quality tracks for your TikTok videos.

Remember to research and evaluate each tool based on your specific needs and budget. These resources can enhance your TikTok marketing efforts and provide valuable assistance in maximizing your success on the platform.

As the TikTok landscape continues to evolve, new tools and platforms may emerge. Stay updated with the latest trends and innovations in TikTok marketing to ensure you're utilizing the most effective tools available. Happy TikTok marketing!

Bonus

If you're looking for inspiration on TikTok, there are several successful accounts that can serve as great examples.

In the world of TikTok, there are countless examples of accounts that have achieved tremendous success and garnered a massive following. These accounts have managed to captivate audiences, showcase creativity, and leverage the unique features of the platform. Let's explore a few examples of successful TikTok accounts:

1. @charlidamelio: Charli D'Amelio is one of the most recognizable names on TikTok. With her energetic dance videos and relatable content, she quickly rose to fame and became one of the platform's top influencers. Charli's authenticity and ability to connect with her audience have helped her amass millions of followers and collaborations with major brands.

2. @mrbeast: MrBeast, also known as Jimmy Donaldson, is a prominent YouTuber who has successfully transitioned to TikTok. His philanthropic stunts, creative challenges, and engaging storytelling have made him a sensation on the platform. With his generous giveaways and unique content ideas, MrBeast has built a loyal following and gained millions of views on his TikTok videos.

3. @addisonre: Addison Rae is another TikTok star who has amassed a massive following. Her dance routines, fashion content, and relatable skits have resonated with TikTok users worldwide. Addison's ability to stay on top of trends and consistently deliver engaging content has helped her become a prominent figure in the TikTok community.

4. @thejasonhorton: Jason Horton is a comedian and content creator who has found success on TikTok. With his humorous skits, comedic commentary, and relatable storytelling, Jason

has managed to build a dedicated following. His ability to tap into trending topics and deliver comedic content has garnered him significant engagement and recognition on the platform.

5. @lizzza: Liza Koshy, a well-known YouTuber and actress, has also found success on TikTok. Her comedic timing, creative editing, and infectious personality have translated well to the platform. Liza's ability to connect with her audience and consistently deliver entertaining content has helped her maintain a strong presence on TikTok.

These are just a few examples of successful TikTok accounts that have achieved widespread recognition and garnered millions of followers. Each of these accounts has its unique style, content approach, and audience engagement strategies. By studying these successful accounts and understanding the elements that contribute to their success, you can gain valuable insights and inspiration for your TikTok marketing efforts.

It's important to note that success on TikTok is not solely measured by the number of followers or views but also by the ability to build genuine connections with the audience, create relatable content, and stay true to your brand identity. By staying consistent, experimenting with different content formats, and engaging with your audience, you can pave the way for your own TikTok success story.

Conclusion

TikTok has emerged as a powerful force in the digital landscape, offering immense opportunities for brands, marketers, and content creators. Throughout this comprehensive guide, we have explored the rise and influence of TikTok, its unique features and user demographics, and its impact on online marketing.

TikTok's exponential growth and global reach have made it a platform that cannot be ignored. By understanding the power of TikTok and its ability to connect with audiences in a new and engaging way, you can harness its potential to boost your brand's online presence.

Creating an effective TikTok marketing strategy is crucial for success on the platform. By defining your brand identity and objectives on TikTok, you can align your content with your overall marketing goals. Identifying and understanding your target audience is key to tailoring your content and ensuring its relevance and appeal.

Crafting compelling content ideas is a crucial aspect of TikTok marketing. By leveraging TikTok's unique features such as effects, sounds, and trends, you can create content that stands out and resonates with your audience. Engaging storytelling, humor, and creativity can help captivate viewers and build a loyal following.

Optimizing your TikTok profile and content is essential for attracting and retaining viewers. By setting up and optimizing your profile, including catchy captions and relevant hashtags, and designing visually appealing videos, you can make a strong impression and increase your chances of going viral.

Understanding TikTok's algorithm and staying updated with the latest trends and challenges are vital for success. By decoding the TikTok algorithm and leveraging its features such as the Discovery Page and For You Page, you can increase your chances of reaching a wider audience. By staying in tune with the latest trends, you can create content that is relevant, relatable, and shareable.

Growing your TikTok following and engagement requires building an authentic community. By fostering engagement through comments, duets, and collaborations, you can create a sense of community and loyalty among your followers. Collaborating with TikTok influencers and creators can also expand your reach and attract new audiences.

Monetizing your TikTok presence is another aspect to explore. By exploring TikTok's monetization options, such as sponsored content and brand partnerships, you can turn your TikTok presence into a source of revenue. Maximizing revenue through TikTok's Creator Fund and livestreaming can further enhance your monetization potential.

Tracking your TikTok analytics and performance is crucial for optimizing your strategy. By utilizing TikTok's analytics tools, you can gain insights into your video performance, audience engagement, and follower demographics. This data-driven approach allows you to refine your content strategy and make informed decisions.

TikTok advertising and paid promotions offer additional avenues for reaching your target audience. By understanding the different ad formats, setting up effective ad campaigns, targeting specific audiences, and analyzing ad performance, you can maximize your advertising ROI on TikTok.

Throughout this guide, we have also explored inspiring TikTok success stories and case studies. These examples have highlighted the potential of

TikTok to elevate brands and individuals to new heights. By learning from these success stories and analyzing different approaches for various goals, you can gain valuable insights and inspiration for your own TikTok marketing journey.

As we look to the future, it's important to embrace new features and formats on TikTok. TikTok is constantly evolving, introducing new tools, effects, and features. By staying ahead of the curve and exploring cross-platform integration and collaboration, you can leverage the latest advancements to enhance your TikTok marketing efforts.

TikTok presents a wealth of opportunities for brands, marketers, and content creators. By embracing TikTok's power, creativity, and vibrant community, you can boost your brand's online presence, engage with a global audience, and drive meaningful results. So, get ready to make your mark on TikTok and propel your marketing efforts to new heights in 2023 and beyond!

Congratulations!

You are now equipped with the knowledge and strategies to navigate the exciting world of TikTok marketing in 2023. As TikTok continues to evolve, it's essential to stay adaptable, creative, and in tune with your audience. Embrace the power of TikTok and its vibrant community to drive brand awareness, engagement, and growth.

Get ready to make your mark on TikTok and propel your marketing efforts to new heights in 2023 and beyond!

www.ingramcontent.com/pod-product-compliance
Lightning Source LLC
Chambersburg PA
CBHW060852220526
45466CB00003B/1342